D0487158

Pip

I've got elephants, tiny little elephants,
hardly any bigger than ʌ̶ɴ̶ ̶ᴀ̶ɴ̶ᴅ̶ ̶ᴏ̶ɴ̶ ̶ᴀ̶ ̶ʙ̶ᴏx.

I've got elephants, tiny little elephants,
and every single elephant belongs to me.

Have you read Tony Mitton's
other fantastic poetry books:

Plum

"*Plum* is a first collection by Tony Mitton and it's a
treat ... here is a book by a man who likes writing poetry
and wants his readers to enjoy it, too."

Lindsey Fraser, Guardian

"*Plum* is so good a debut collection that Tony Mitton
might just be the next Charles Causley of children's
poetry."

Times Educational Supplement

The Red and White
Spotted Handkerchief

"Tony Mitton's second collection of children's verse,
The Red and White Spotted Handkerchief, more than lives
up to the promise of his first book, *Plum.* If you buy only
one volume of children's poetry this year, let it be this
handsomely jacketed and illustrated narrative sequence."

Michael Thorn, Literary Review

Pip

Tony Mitton

Illustrated by
Peter Bailey

SCHOLASTIC
PRESS

Scholastic Children's Books,
Commonwealth House, 1-19 New Oxford Street,
London, WC1A 1NU, UK
a division of Scholastic Ltd
London ~ New York ~ Toronto ~ Sydney ~ Auckland
Mexico City ~ New Delhi ~ Hong Kong

First published by Scholastic Ltd, 2001
This edition published by Scholastic Ltd, 2002

Copyright © Tony Mitton, 2001
Illustrations copyright © Peter Bailey, 2001

ISBN 0 439 98165 4

Printed by WS Bookwell, Finland

10 9 8 7 6 5 4 3 2 1

The rights of Tony Mitton and Peter Bailey to be identified as the
author and illustrator of this work respectively have been asserted by them
in accordance with the Copyright, Designs and Patents Act, 1988.

To Ben Duncan and Dick Chapman
and to little pips everywhere
T. M.

For Ness, who designed it
P. B.

Contents

Grown Out Of

My trousers are tight.
They just won't fit.

And my jumper?
I've grown out of it.

My shirt's too short.
It just won't do.

There are holes in my socks
where my toes peep through.

So it's lucky I don't
grow out of my skin.

'Cos then there'd be nothing
to put me in.

Gregory's Pet

Gregory the Giant
got a dragon for a pet.
The dragon didn't grow
so he took it to the vet.

The vet said, "Well now,
let me see…"
Then he took a rubber hammer
and he tapped it on the knee.

He clicked on his torch,
as he muttered, "Open wide."
And, carefully and thoughtfully,
he peered inside.

"Does he eat his boulders?
Does he chew his wood?
Does he drink his rivers
like a healthy dragon should?

"What! No boulders?
Eh? None at all?
Well! No wonder
he's this small!"

But the vet bent down
and he took a closer look.
Then he went to his desk
and he riffled through a book.

"No, I think," said the vet,
as he squinted in its ear,
"that a grass-eating dragon
is what we have here."

"And that," said the vet,
as he peered up its nose,
"means, if it gets grass,
it grows and grows."

So Gregory the Giant
led his dragon-pet away
to leave it on his castle lawn,
day by day.

Yes, he left it to nibble
and munch and chew,
and gradually his dragon
just grew and grew.

And that's how his dragon,
the size of a sheep,
became so big
that Greg gave a leap. . .

He landed on its back
and it soared so high
the two of them went
       cloud-cruising,
off across the sky.

The Snap Gap

Between the carpet
and the mat
is a dark and shiny
floorboard gap.
It looks like water,
shining so,
and if you put
down one small foot,
or even just
one little toe,
the crocodile
will come and snap.
So do not tread
upon the gap.
No, do not step
and do not stop.
Just jump
and take
a little hop.

Land lightly,
slightly.
Do not bump.
And sneak across,
yes, creep away,
and then the croc
will stay asleep,
it may…

I Can

I can move lightly,
light as a feather.

I can move
free as a leaf
blown by the weather.

I can reach right up
to tickle the sky.

I can curl tight
as an insect's eye.

I can spread out
in the shape of a star.

And I can **JUMP**!
See how far…

Frog Hops 1

One hop, two hop,
I'm a little frog.

Three hop, four hop,
bopping on a log.

Five hop, six hop,
that's the way to bop.

Seven hop, eight hop,
Wheeeeee ... PLOP!

Frog Hops 2

One hop, two hop,
I'm a grubby frog.

Three hop, four hop,
slopping on a log.

Five hop, six hop,
I need a little wash.

Seven hop, eight hop,
Wheeeeee ... SPLOSH!

Sweet Song

(Granny's Skipping Rhyme)

I like liquorice.
I like lollipops.
I like stopping
at the old sweet shop.

I like peppermints.
I like sugarsticks.
I like bubblegum…
                POP!

(note: jump out on "POP!")

Tooth Fairies

Sometimes I wonder,
what is the truth?
What do the fairies
do with a tooth?

Perhaps they buy
those tiny bones
to shape them into
shiny thrones.

Or take each white tooth
lightly down
to carve a curious,
gleaming crown.

Maybe they cut them
square and slick
to build a wall
that's sheer and thick.

Or take up neat
and nimble tools
to trim them into
necklace jewels.

But who can tell
or understand
what takes place
in fairyland
with secret skill
of fairy hand?

The Cave

Can you be daring?
Can you be brave?
Will you come down
to explore the cave?

We'll put on our boots
and carefully tramp
down through the slippery
dark and damp.

They say there's a chest
a hundred years old.
It's spilling over
with jewels and gold.

The pirates left it
and never returned.
Their ship caught fire
and the map got burned.

So I'll take the torch
and you take the sack.
Let's go down there
and bring some back.

But hush! There's a dragon
who just might waken,
if he hears any of it
being taken.

Elefantasy

I've got elephants, tiny little
  elephants,
hardly any bigger than an ant
  or a bee.

I've got elephants, tiny little
  elephants,
and every single elephant belongs
  to me.

I've got elephants, tiny little
  elephants,
peeping from my pockets and hiding
  in my hair.

I've got elephants, but nobody can
  see them.
I'm the only person who knows
  they're there.

Mmmmmm…

Cows in a meadow in summer
munching on juicy grass –
milk in a glass.

Corn in a sea of tossing gold
with the sun high overhead –
freshly baked bread.

Hen with its broody cluck
strutting on jerky legs –
new-laid eggs.

Brambles with clustering berries
under a blue sky –
Mmmmmm ... warm pie.

For David Fickling
T. M.

The Woodcutter's Daughter

There once was a woodcutter
lived in a wood.
His young daughter Mary
was gentle and good.
But the little girl's mother
was buried and dead.
And a stepmother stood
in her place now, instead.

The stepmother came
with a child of her own,
whose heart, like her mother's,
was cold as the stone.
When the woodcutter took up
his axe and went out,
the mother and daughter
would grumble and shout,

"Oh Mary, come quickly,
and clean up the sink.
Now stitch up my stockings
and fetch me a drink.
Then clean out the fireplace
and sweep up the floor,
and wash all the windows
and polish the door."

They'd boss and they'd bully.
They'd rant and they'd moan.
And Mary felt miserable,
sad and alone.
But Mary grew pretty
and graceful and tall,
and the woodcutter loved her
the best of them all.

Now this made the others
hate Mary the worse,
so the stepmother gritted
her teeth in a curse,
"I'll set her a task
in the depths of the wood,
a task that will rid us
of Mary for good!"

It was deep in the winter,
with snow all around,
and everything frozen,
yes, even the ground.
The stepmother led Mary
out to the gate,
then she uttered these words
in a mouthful of hate,

"Gather me strawberries,
juicy red strawberries,
out in the wilderness,
deep in the snow.
Never come back
till you've gathered such strawberries.
Pick up your basket
and go!"

Poor Mary went quietly,
off on her way.
She could not resist,
so she had to obey.
She knew that no berries
could grow in that cold.
But her stepmother's hate
made her do as was told.

She walked through the wilderness,
chilly and white,
as the day drained away
to the darkness of night.
She thought that her life
would be lost in that dark,
when suddenly hope
lighted up like a spark!

For there, through the trees,
she saw orange and gold.
"A fire," she murmured,
"to keep out the cold."
There were folk round the fire,
all warming themselves.
And to Mary's surprise
it was twelve little elves!

"Now Mary," said one,
"don't be shy, never fear.
Our fire will warm you.
Be bold and draw near.
We're the elves of the months,
and we know who you are.
If it's berries you seek,
then you need not go far.

"My brother July will soon
fill up your basket…
You see – it is done! You had
barely to ask it.
Your basket is brimful
of strawberries red.
Now my brother will lead you
straight back to your bed."

July chose a fire-coal,
glowing and bright,
then he led Mary back
through the depths of the night.
But when she returned,
though her stepmother smiled,
her eyes seemed to glitter
so bitter and wild.

So the next time the woodcutter
went on his way,
Mary's stepmother called her
to smile and to say,
"Go out through the snow, Mary.
Take a long ramble.
And find us some blackberries,
ripe on the bramble:

"Gather me blackberries,
purple, plump blackberries,
out in the wilderness,
far in the snow.
Never come back
till you've gathered such blackberries.
Pick up your basket
and go!"

Well, Mary went quickly,
for this time she knew
just where she could go,
and indeed what to do.
For she knew that the elves
would assist in her task.
She had only to go
to their fire and ask.

She walked till she spied
the bright glow of the fire.
And this time the flames
seemed to crackle yet higher.
Then up got the leader with,
"Mary, my dear,
you've come for your blackberries.
Look. They are here."

October said, "Truly.
Believe it, my child."
And Mary's big basket
was instantly piled.
The blackberries glistened
so plump and so fine,
and the juice trickled out of them
darkly as wine.

October then picked out
a coal, big and bright,
and led Mary home
by the glow of its light.
But when Mary's stepmother
saw her return,
the hate in her heart
made her bristle and burn.

"Now, tell me your secret,
for fruit will not grow
in the wintery wastes
of the ice and the snow."
So Mary then spoke
of the twelve little elves
who sat round their fire,
all warming themselves.

"You foolish young wastrel!
Those twelve little men
are told of in stories
again and again.
You could have had rubies
as red as ripe cherries!
You could have brought jewels.
And yet you've brought berries.

"Now, show us the way,
and my daughter and I
will seek out the place
where that fire leaps high.
We'll wish from those elf-men
a pile of treasure,
and then we'll return
to a life full of pleasure."

So Mary then pointed,
and watched them both go,
like little black beetles
across the white snow.
And away they both went
to that fire so bright,
where the flames seemed to whip
at the edge of the night.

The leader approached
from the rim of the fire.
"Now what is your wish?"
he began to inquire.
"We wish to have silver.
We wish to have gold.
As much as our baskets
can possibly hold."

The leader could hear
the greed in her voice.
"And so," he commanded,
"you *shall* have your choice."
He called out to March, and said,
"Take them to where
the gold of the sunset
bleeds over the air.

"And then take them up
to the dark, hollow night,
where the needle-like stars
prick their silvery light.
There's an endless supply
of both silver and gold,
much more than their baskets
can possibly hold."

So March raised his wind
and it whirled them away
to gather the gold
from the end of the day,
then up to the darkness,
so high and so far,
to sift out the silver
from star upon star.

But, whether they ever
completed their task,
they never came back,
so it's fruitless to ask.
Perhaps they still grasp
at the glittering air,
with the cold in their hearts
and the wind in their hair.

While the humble old woodcutter,
here in the wood,
with Mary his daughter,
so gentle and good,
live simply and happily,
ever and after,
warming their cottage
with love and with laughter.

And what of the blaze
with the twelve little men?
They're out in the forest
till needed again.

The End

Fire

Fire flits lightly
in fingery flames.

Fire plays
flickery games.

Fire frolics
and twists
and turns.

Watch out!
Whatever it touches
fire burns.

But fire sighs,
settling,
into a whispery sleep,

under its quilt of ash
in a crumpled heap.

Voices of Water

The water in the rain says
                    Tick Tick Tack
The water in the sleet says
                    Slush
The water in the ice says
                    Crick Crick Crack
The water in the snow says
                    Hush

The water in the sink says
                    Slosh Slosh
The water in the tap says
                    Drip
The water in the bath says
                    Wash Wash
The water in the cup says
                    Sip

The water in the pool says

                Splish Splash

The water in the stream says

                Trill

The water in the sea says

                Crish Crash

The water in the pond …

                stays still.

The water in the soil says

                Sow, Sow

The water in the cloud says

                Give

The water in the plant says

                Grow, Grow

The water in the world says

                Live

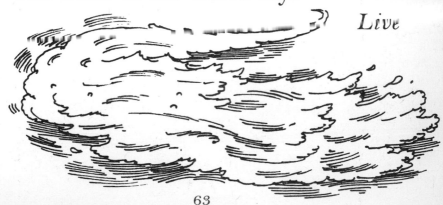

My Snowman

My snowman is standing
out on the lawn.
His hat is battered.
His gloves are torn.

My snowman is silent,
cold and alone.
His heart is ice.
His eyes are stone.

My snowman is melting.
He trickles away,
out in a world
so chill and grey.

I'll make him again,
I will, one day.

My Ball

My ball
just won't bounce
at all.

Not off
the pavement.

Nor off
the wall.

I've tried:
kicking it,
flicking it,
rolling it,
bowling it,
swinging it,
flinging it,
dropping it,
and whopping it!

But it just goes
FLUMP
like a flabby lump.

I'm thinking
of swapping it.

Emergencies

Red Alert! Red Alert!
I've dropped my lolly in the dirt.

S.O.S! S.O.S!
I've spilled some custard
down my dress.

999! 999!
I've ridden my bike
through the washing line.

Ring the alarm! Ring the alarm!
There's an insect landing
on my arm.

Bring First Aid!
Bring First Aid!
There's a beetle in
my lemonade.

Ambulance! And make it quick!
I think I'm going to be sick.

Make a Face

I can make a fat face,
a dog face, a cat face.

I can make a thin face,
a skinny little pin face.

I can make a mad face,
a horrid mean and bad face,

a sick face, a sad face,
a rather like my dad face.

I can make a funny face,
a just as sweet as honey face.

I can make a happy face,
a sharp snarl and snappy face.

I can make a true face,
a just for me and you face.

But *this* face,
you ain't seen *this* face ...

NO PLACE!

Rickety Train Ride

I'm riding the train to Ricketywick.
Clickety clickety clack.
I'm sat in my seat
with a sandwich to eat
as I travel the trickety track.

It's an ever so rickety trickety train,
and I honestly thickety think
that before it arrives
at the end of the line
it will tip up my drippety drink.

On My Island

On my island
you can see
a hut, a boat
and a coconut tree,
bright blue ocean,
golden sand
and laughing waves
that lap the land.

On my island
I only need
some bits and bobs
and a book to read,
a cooking pot,
a dish and spoon,
and a whistle to play
beneath the moon.

Close beside me,
there's a friend
to help me play
at *Let's Pretend*,
someone to say,
"We'll take a trip
and follow the trail
of the Mystery Ship!"

If we go
on an island raid,
we'll come back
with lemonade,
chocolate biscuits,
a currant bun,
and maybe a comic
to read for fun.

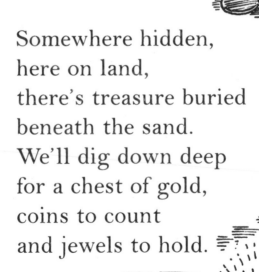

Somewhere hidden,
here on land,
there's treasure buried
beneath the sand.
We'll dig down deep
for a chest of gold,
coins to count
and jewels to hold.

But in the water
we'd better watch out.
Sometimes the Shark
comes swimming about.
We can see its shadow
and its sharp grey fin.
It'll bite our feet
if we dip them in.

Around this island
there's so much sea.
It shimmers with ocean
            mystery,
with mermaid music
and magic tides,
underwater wonders
and dolphin rides.

And down by the shore
are ragged rocks
where merfolk come
to comb their locks,
to sit by the tide
and trim their tails,
and gather seaweed
to scrub their scales.

Across the water
is another isle.
Its people sing
and laugh and smile.
They ask us over
to dance and play.
Then they wave us home
at the end of the day.

Over my island
sleeps the sky
where comets flash
and the moon rides high.
As we lie and swing
in our hammock bed
we can see them sparkling
overhead.

On my island
there's sea and sun,
plenty to do
and lots of fun.
So use this map
to find your way.
Jump in a boat
and come today!

Worm Words

"Keep still!"
said Big Worm
to Little Worm.
"You're driving me
round the bend."

"Don't be daft,"
said Little Worm.
"I'm your other end."

Minibeast Movements

This is the way the beetle stumbles,
clumsy, clockwork, slow.

This is the way the grasshopper leaps,
so! so! so!

This is the way the snail slides,
smooth, steady, sure.

And this is the way the
          spider scuttles,
swiftly across the floor!

Insect

Inspect
an insect
and you'll see
how perfect
it can be.

Listen,
and hear
the tiny song
it sings,

as bits of rainbow
glisten
on its wings.

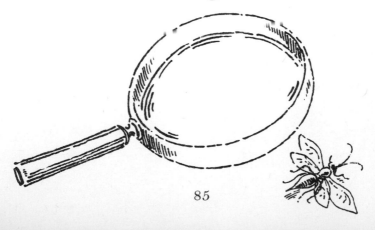

The Matchbox
Monster

The Matchbox Monster is so very
  small
you'd hardly think it was a monster
  at all.
But if you examine its gnashing jaws,
and if you inspect its flashing claws,
and if you consider its crashing roars,
I reckon in the end you're bound to
  agree
it's more like a monster than you or
  me.

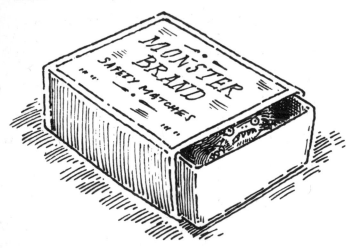

The Matchbox Monster is fond of
  me.
It sits on the edge of my plate at tea.
It rubs its hands and licks its lips.
It sips my milk and nibbles my chips.
It clears up my crumbs and shares
  my dessert.
Then it wipes its mouth on the sleeve
  of my shirt.

The Matchbox Monster likes to float
around my bath in a plastic boat.
It loves to leap from my island knee
to make a splash with a loud, shrill
  "Wheeeeeee!"

The Matchbox Monster sleeps in my
  bed,
snug in its matchbox, close to my
  head.
It shares my story, then tucks up
  tight,
winks one red eye and growls,
  "Goodnight."

Home

The lights are on
in my little house,
and I've cleared away the tea.

My slippers are there
beside the chair,
and they're waiting just for me.

The cat's curled up
on the sofa,
in a softly purring heap.

So soon I'll take
my book to bed,
and read myself to sleep.

Listening in Bed

As I listen hard
in bed tonight,

I can hear
the floor creak,
the door squeak,
the tap leak.

I can hear
the dishes clink
down in the kitchen sink.

I can hear
the telly boom
down in the sitting room.

And very near
I can hear
my little brother
breathing deep.

Sssssh…
He's fast asleep.

Blood Beast

What's that whining,
there in the night?
It must be the creature
with the terrible bite.

It flies through the air
like a vampire beast.
It wants your blood
for a midnight feast.

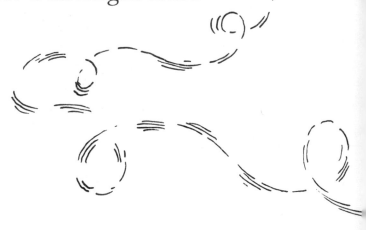

So hide your head,
fold up your feet
and tuck yourself tightly
under your sheet...

It'll get you in the end
wherever you go.
You can't escape
from the mosquieeeeeeeeeeeee...
*No! It's landing on my **toe**!*

Clumsy Giant
Gets Up

Clumsy Giant fell out of bed.
He reached for his slippers and
  bumped his head.

He stomped to the bathroom to wash
  his face,
and slopped hot water all over the
  place.

He searched for his clothes with a
  grumbly grunt.
Then he heaved on his T-shirt,
  back-to-front.

He found his trousers and gave a
  shout.
Then he pulled them on quickly,
  inside-out.
He scrabbled about with a mumbly
  sound,
and put on his boots, the wrong way
  round.

He clomped to the mirror to brush
  his hair,
slipped on the carpet and broke a
  chair.

He squeezed his foot and he rubbed
  his head.
"I'll try to be careful now," he said.

So he went quite slowly, to open the
  door,
tripped on his bootlace and fell on
  the floor.

Clumsy Giant Has Breakfast

Clumsy Giant went downstairs
to make his morning snack.
He skidded on the kitchen floor
and landed on his back.

Clumsy Giant tried to pour
his cornflakes out with care.
But then he sneezed! And clumsy
  cornflakes
scattered everywhere.

Clumsy Giant poured the milk
as well as he was able.
He saw a spider, gave a shriek,
and spilled it on the table.

Clumsy Giant spread his toast
with jam, the clever chap!
He picked it up with giant pride
and dropped it in his lap.

Clumsy Giant made a pot
of tea, to cheer him up.
He picked it up to pour it out
and went and missed the cup.

"Perhaps I'll have some pancakes.
I'm good at those," he said.
He flipped the first one in the air...
It landed on his head.

Tiny Diny

Dear, oh dear,
oh, what shall I do?
There's a tiny little dinosaur
in my shoe.

Her teeth are sharp
and her head's like a rock.
When I put my foot in,
she chewed my sock.

Her skin is rough
and her tail is long.
And her ripply muscles
look ever so strong.

And I want to go out,
but what can I do
with a tiny little dinosaur
in my shoe?

One Day
(when I grow up)

One day,
when I grow up,
I'll take a trip.

I'll hop on a bus
(no fuss!)
then take a ship.

The ship will sail me
far away ...
but not just now,
no, not today.

For now,
I think I'll stay.

But one day,
when I grow up,
I'll travel far.

I'll jump in a car
and say, *"Ta-ra!"*
Then take a train
or p'raps a plane.

The plane will fly me
through the air
and then I'll end up,
well ... *somewhere*.

Yes, one day,
when I grow up,
I'll travel round the
world.
That's the life for me.

But just for now,
I think I'll stay at home.

You see…
I'm only three.

Besides,
it's nearly time for tea.

Pip

Take a tip, pip.

Listen to a word
from a lip, pip.

Find what's found
in the ground.

Don't look back.

Let your shell
crack.

Reach out a root.

Send up a shoot.

Look round for room
to grow and bloom.

Then take a trip, pip.

Index of first lines